S0-BPN-057

DIVIDED

D I V I

OTHER TITLES BY LINDA FRANK

Cobalt Moon Embrace

Insomnie Blues

Kahlo: The World Split Open

DED

LINDA FRANK

© LINDA FRANK, 2018

No part of this publication may be reproduced, stored in a retrieval system or transmitted, in any form or by any means, without the prior written consent of the publisher or a license from the Canadian Copyright Licensing Agency (Access Copyright). For an Access Copyright license, visit www.accesscopyright.ca or call toll free to 1-800-893-5777.

James Street North Books is an imprint of Wolsak and Wynn Publishers.

Cover and interior design: Natalie Olsen, Kisscut Design
Cover image from *Insects abroad : being a popular account of foreign insects, their structure, habits, and transformations* by J.G. Wood (1883)
Author photograph: Caitlin Burgess
Typeset in Quant
Printed by Coach House Printing Company Toronto, Canada

The publisher gratefully acknowledges the support of the Canada Council for the Arts, the Ontario Arts Council and the Government of Canada.

James Street North Books
280 James Street North
Hamilton, Ontario
Canada L8R 2L3

Library and Archives Canada Cataloguing in Publication
Frank, Linda, author
Divided / Linda Frank.
Poems.
ISBN 978-1-928088-58-5 (softcover)
I. Title.
PS8561.R2777D58 2018   C811'.6   C2018-900525-4

As always, for Ken, Allison and Caitlin

CONTENTS

I   STRANGE CREATURES

Divided 3

Jewel Wasp 4

Praying Mantis 5

Dragonfly 6

Swarm 7

Training Your Cricket to Be a Warrior 8

Jesus Bugs 10

Orb Weaver 11

Ocean Quahog 12

Nabokov's Blues 13

Darwin's Orchid 14

Firefly 15

Papillon de Nuit 16

Ballooning Spiders 17

The Art of Deception 18

Seventeen 19

Flit 20

Gift 21

II   NIGHT MIGRATION

Origin 25

A Philosophy of Zoos 26

Cage 27

Capture 28

Flea Circus 29

The Language of Bees 30

Von Frisch's *Ten Little Housemates* 31

The Plume Trade 32

Torishima 34

Silkworm 35

Night Migration 36

III **SO FULL OF GHOSTS**

Ascent 41

Show Me God, Hidden in the Stars 44

Falling Stars 45

Descent 46

Half Mile Down 49

The Glanville Fritillary 50

The Carpenter's Daughter 51

They Never Asked Any Questions 53

Silence 54

A Crack in the World 56

Saving the Whooping Crane 58

Old Women in the Sea 59

Maria Sibylla Merian Brings a Brandied Crocodile to Tea 60

IV **HOW MORTAL THEY WERE**

Envoy 71

Red 72

Metamorphosis 73

Where the Sidewalk Ends 74

The Kranstein Forest 75

Frog 76

Morning Glory 77

Terrarium 78

Ginkgo 79

Tadpoles 80

Musca Domestica 81

Sweet 82

Whitefish 83

Tulips 84

Mayfly 86

Acknowledgements 89

Notes 91

I

STRANGE
CREATURES

DIVIDED

Insect from Latin *insectum (animal)* means *divided (animal)* or *cut into sections*

He tells me how much he hates them.
        He shivers when he flicks on the light
and cockroaches tear across
                his floor. Squirms when silverfish
scuttle round the drain of his tub.

Insects fly at you, he says. They crawl up your legs
        buzz at the screen. They bite. Feed
                on your blood. If he could bring himself
to touch them, he'd lash out
                and crush them.

I know they're strange creatures. They breathe
        without lungs. Their blood flows freely
through their body cavity, no veins
                or arteries. No ears. Eyes
on either side of their head. They see
                mosaic images
wear their skeletons on the outside.

How alien they are to him, yet how deeply present
        to me. And how divided we are
                about their place in our world.

JEWEL WASP

She delivers her first sting into his midsection
      and his front legs buckle. The blood-red

thighs of her second and third pair of legs flash
      her beauty. She twists her metallic

emerald body around him, glitters with captured
      light, wrestles her way to his head, slips

her stinger through his exoskeleton, injects
      her venom directly into his brain

probing until she reaches the sweet spot.
      She hijacks his will to move, pulls

on his antenna, leads him back to her burrow
      like a dog on a leash. She needs

his cockroach life, will lay her white egg
      on his live abdomen, block the exit

from her den with pebbles. He can only lie there
      while her larva hatches, watch it

chew a hole in his side and consume
      his internal organs one by one

to keep him
      alive the longest.

PRAYING MANTIS

It's a small sacrifice to make
isn't it? The male loses his head
        to ensure the future.

He's a slave to his hormones
and the nervous system in his abdomen.
        The sensoria in his brain

inhibit him. When he loses
his head, all control is lost.
        He can perform.

The female waits in a posture
of supplication, her pincers
        poised for action.

Her head swivels three hundred
degrees, her huge eyes track
        her moving lover.

DRAGONFLY

The Devil's darning needle, ear sewer, eye poker, ear cutter,
        eye snatcher. Horse stinger. Troll's spindle.
                The adder's servant, it follows
snakes around and stitches them up when they are injured.

August god, lady of the weeping willow, widow skimmer,
        water witch. The Devil's little horse sent by Satan
                to create chaos

                        to steal people's souls.

SWARM

They behave the way they must.

The eighth of ten plagues. The Pharaoh feared
       only the threat of darkness
              and death of the first-born more.

Nymphs gather
       in millions and begin to march, joined
in their advance by millions
          more, until they merge

into one long column covering tens of miles
       all of them proceeding in a straight line.
          And as they march, they shed

their final skin, become fully winged adults
       and take to the air, a massive shadow
             falling over the world.

In blind collective instinct, they swarm.

Locusts, slippery and slick, carpet hundreds
       of square miles, strip every plant
and crop in their path, devour
         every tree. Bare branches
break under the weight of them.

They eat anything green. Grass, grapevines, green
       paint off walls and water tanks, green clothes
hanging on a washing line. Plastics and textiles.
        Their fallen comrades. Only
          what's underground is safe.

Choose your cricket by body colour. Yellow crickets
are the most aggressive, but green insects, *qing*,
are more strategic.

Consider the energy of the antennae, the colour
of its eyebrows, the thickness of its feet,
the strength of its jaw.

The skin must be dry and reflect light from inside itself.
Strength is more important than size. The quality
of the jaw is decisive.

A cricket knows when it is loved and will respond
with the Five Virtues, human qualities found
in the best warrior crickets.

When it is time to sing he will sing. This is trustworthiness.
The cricket will hold its wings like an acoustical sail.
His chirp can goad his enemy.

Learn to provoke the cricket by stroking its jaw
with pencil-thin yard grass straw
or a mouse whisker.

On meeting an enemy, he will not hesitate to fight.
This is courage. You and your cricket must understand
each other in a language beyond words.

Even seriously wounded, he will not surrender.
This is loyalty. The cricket is a warrior.
The winners are generals.

A defeated cricket will not protest the outcome
of a fight. He will accept defeat and leave the arena
without bluster or complaint.

When defeated, he will not sing. He knows no shame.
Release your vanquished cricket back into nature.
He is protected by a curse against any who would harm him.

When he becomes cold, he will return to his home.
He is wise and understands his situation.

Remember there has been a deep history between people
and crickets. Their singing has kept our loneliness away.

Learn the Three Reversals that recognize the differences
between humans and crickets.

Ask how are you and your warrior cricket similar yet different?
Ask how something can be one thing and another at the same time?

JESUS BUGS

Striders live upon
      reflection. An aquatic
            glissade. Skip like rain.

Is the sky water

            or the water sky?

At night they spider
      dance on the milky way.
                Hunt their living prey.

ORB WEAVER

Surrounded, detached, in measureless oceans of space,
Ceaselessly musing, venturing, throwing, seeking the spheres to connect them,
Till the bridge you will need be form'd, till the ductile anchor hold,
Till the gossamer thread you fling catch somewhere, O my soul.
WALT WHITMAN, "A Noiseless Patient Spider"

Ceaselessly musing, venturing, throwing, seeking the spheres to
      connect them
The diaphanous filament you float on the wind
Till the gossamer thread you fling catch somewhere, O my soul
The dragline and the drop line

The diaphanous filament you float on the wind
Your slow folding and unfolding of legs
The dragline and the drop line
My presence of no concern to you

Your slow folding and unfolding of legs
You weave between the branches of the cedar
My presence of no concern to you
You weave, and the sunlight shines the threads silver

You weave between the branches of the cedar
Till the bridge you will need be form'd, till the ductile anchor hold
You weave, and the sunlight shines the threads silver
Surrounded, detached, in measureless oceans of space

OCEAN QUAHOG

They named it Ming. An ancient creature
      each growth line on its polished surface
            a record of the four centuries it lived
      fastened to the ocean floor.

The oldest living animal on earth. Still alive
      when they sliced through its mahogany shell
            counted its four hundred and five rings.

NABOKOV'S BLUES

i.

Wings folded, they are grey
bits, tiny triangles sprinkled with black pepper.

Wings open, they are Pygmy blues
the size of a shirt button.

Not even his love could save them.

ii.
A love begun in childhood. A passion turned
into insane joy for the hunt.

To distinguish one from the other
to tell them apart.
No one had.

iii.
His beloved blues.

Xerces blue, gone from the sand dunes
of San Francisco. Lotis blue, gone
from the California coast.

Karner blue, silvery and dark. He found it, named
it, called himself its godfather.

It still holds out, clinging, like his love
in dwindling colonies in the Northeast.

DARWIN'S ORCHID

i.
Its throat implausibly long. Creamy white
        waxy star on a stem that gives rise to a fan
                of leathery jade leaves. Its nectar
found at the bottom of a spur that dangles
        ten inches below the flower's lip.
                It blooms once a year
                        in winter.

A flower once believed a creation of magic.

ii.
        But Darwin envisioned a moth,
a moth with a proboscis long enough to pollinate
        the Madagascar orchid.
                He died still believing.

iii.
Drawn through the dark forest by the scent
        of the stark white orchid
finally caught on film with infrared light
        more than a century after Darwin's death

        the night-flying hawk moth unfurls its tongue in the jungle.

FIREFLY

A jewelled lucifer, the winged beetle holds
  its cold bright sparkle to its belly.
Each flash a mating song of light.

Caravaggio prepared his canvas with a powder
  of dried fireflies, a master
      of chiaroscuro.

          You told me you wanted to own things.
Your place at the bar. Your seat on the bus, the corner
      of the street where you live.
You said you needed to feel as if you were in control.

Fireflies stop their flickering when they are captured.
  They leave their light on
      and this makes us love them more.

We keep them in jars. Don't provide food and water.
  Deprive them of oxygen.
      They don't survive the night.

PAPILLON DE NUIT

I caught you in a meadow of violet
        and raspberry, a butterfly in the morning
             light, navigating by the sun.
                            You spun
and your wings broke the light in colour prisms, so beautiful
        I wanted to capture you, pin you to me forever.

You stole my sleep and I turned into a creature
        of darkness, restless in my muslin husk, guided
by celestial light in the nocturnal sky. The beauty
             of my wings, hidden by night.

And as a moth does, I wanted to drink your tears, slip
        under your eyelids as you slept.
                         Your nights
were peaceful. You roused from your chrysalis
        into the break of day, but your iridescence
             was a trick of scattering light.

Moths are not drawn to the flame, only fooled
        by it. They have no choice. They plummet
             in a spiral flight path closer
        and closer to that consuming light.

BALLOONING SPIDERS

All around us, they climbed
        to the tip of a twig, a blade of grass
stood on tiptoe, and angled their abdomens
        to the sky, casting themselves
                up into the heavens.

That summer we lay on our backs in fields
        of buttercup, yarrow and daisy
                watching them. The blue
blue sky filled with their gossamer flight.

We believed we too could fly away

like those tiny octagon parachutes
        riding the thermal wind.

At seventeen we had the urge
        for going, believed nothing stayed
                in one place

and that some things
        would never belong anywhere.

THE ART OF DECEPTION

Like the wings of the electric blue morpho, you
    are iridescent, your underwings dark.

When the morpho flies through flickering light
    in the forest or slides across the slice of sun
        in a meadow, it seems to disappear.

When last we spoke, you promised to call again soon
    to tell me everything. Months and months
        and nothing. Today, your voice
            as if no time had passed.

The green hairstreak mistaken for a leaf, the hoary
    comma swallowed by a tree trunk. They
        camouflage themselves to survive.

Perhaps true deception is not about disappearance
    but the capacity to reappear, the sudden
        replacement of one presence by another.

SEVENTEEN

Australians have the best names for them you said –
yellow Monday, chocolate soldier, blue moon,
cherry nose, whiskey drinker, tiger prince

floury baker, golden emperor, sand grinder,
green whizzer, black prince, bagpipe,
razor grinder, green grocer and double drummer.

Such great names. You didn't want to leave any out.

We were lying on our backs in the tall grass beside the flagpole
challenging each other to stare into the sun, to see
who would be the first to turn away.

The cicadas were tuning up after seventeen years underground, like rusty
wheels of a freight train screeching a metal track
a chorus of broken violins bowed by a handsaw
the rising whine of electrical wires gone nuclear.

When cicadas moult into adults, you whisper, they abandon
their skins and leave their empty husks for us
clinging to the bark of trees.

FLIT

Chuang Tzu dreamt he became a butterfly
and on waking, the butterfly became Chuang Tzu.

When I close my eyes, orange throbs
against turquoise behind my eyelids, like monarchs undulating

over Lake Huron, where last week I spent
humid August days chasing the late summer orange flit

of the milkweed butterflies. Stalked them at the water's edge
in the thistles and goldenrod, blue flag and loosestrife

to collect their image with my camera, that desire
to have and to keep.

Now in the city I wonder about transformation
about insects that shed their exoskeletons, leave empty
replicas of themselves behind.

GIFT

Shafts of light slice shadows
        between fir trees. Tiny balloon flies glisten
            swarm the sunbeams
approach each other in the air and embrace.

The male courts the female, offers her
        gifts before they mate.

His first offering a dead juicy insect, his next a corpse
        sucked dry and wrapped in brilliant white tissue
            and his final gift, a carefully woven
empty silken silver balloon.

As if you'd first wooed me with diamonds, then
        with the wrapping paper covering the diamonds and won
            my hand in marriage with the empty box.

I remove your ring from my finger. Place it
        in the palm of your hand. Above our heads
            the secrets of small flies
                and their shiny gifts.

NIGHT
MIGRATION

ORIGIN

They call him the Devil's chaplain.
     They say he killed God.
But those years on the *Beagle* sometimes felt
as if we were in the Garden of Eden, swimming
     in coral lagoons, riding through tropical forests
full of birds, lying on our backs under a sky
        rich with stars up in the Andes.
I swear God was all around us.

And the time we were in the Galapagos,
all those iguanas, giant tortoises, mockingbirds, boobies.
     He was in awe, so close to a hawk he could touch it.

He was always collecting – birds, animals, sea creatures,
     insects, fossils, ricks and plants.
       He trained himself to *see.*

I shot that bird for the cooking pot, the bird half eaten
     when he realized it was the unknown species
he'd been searching for, the rhea,
     some sort of South American ostrich.

He said this was the moment he knew creation
     didn't make sense. There had to be some sort
of evolution, a common origin, even for humans.

Captain FitzRoy was a Christian man
     and he took that young Darwin on a voyage
that destroyed the idea God made every one of us.

Monotheism drove them from the ancient
    temple, replaced the horse goddess Epona,
        the golden calf, the jaguar, the veneration

of every large and potent animal species
    with the worship of an abstract god. Animal
        demoted to demon.

How then, to experience the holy shiver?
    How to look into the eyes
        of powerful alien beings
            and experience the fear and awe
        we once found there?

CAGE

what is different. Cage what we fear.
Cage them in menageries
                 as exotic spectacle.

Cage them behind bars, in small ramshackle
enclosures, in beast wagons, circus trailers,
                 travelling shows.

Hire agents to collect them.
Trade a pound of salt and a bolt of cloth for one.
          Trap and capture the rest.

Cage them in the Bronx Zoo, the London Zoo,
          in Hamburg and Antwerp, Barcelona, Milan.
                    As late as 1958 in Brussels.

Display one in Piccadilly Circus. Baptize her.
Though her name is Sarah Baartman, call her
          the Hottentot Venus. Sell her

to an animal trainer, and then to French scientists
and when she dies, dissect and dismember her,
          display her skeleton in museums.

Exhibit one in St. Louis and New Orleans
          and then cage him in New York
with a chimpanzee, parrot and orangutan.

Call him Ota Benga, and when you are finished
          gawking, set him free
to put a bullet through his own heart.

CAPTURE

For a fun and rewarding summer activity
indulge your urge to capture a butterfly.

Move slowly. Position a net under the insect
      and swing upwards. Flip it over
and the insect can't escape.

Carefully guide the butterfly down into a killing jar.
Butterflies are fragile. They can batter themselves
      in the killing jar trying to escape.
Stun them by pinching their thorax.
      It takes practise to get this method right.
Practise first on common moths
      that won't concern you if they escape.

Use ethyl acetate to keep the insect soft
      enough to be mounted properly.
But if the butterfly has stiffened in death, you must
      make a relaxing chamber. Cover the butterfly
with two damp paper towels in an airtight plastic
container and close the lid.

The butterfly will soften in two to three days.
Use forceps to remove the butterfly from the killing jar.
      Insert a pin through the right side of the thorax.
Pinch the thorax and as if the butterfly were alive
      the wings will spread flat.
Let the butterfly dry for two weeks, the same time
      it takes a chrysalis to produce an imago.

Display your butterflies in a glass-covered box.
      Mount the insects on foam board
with special insect pins and remember
      your collection has scientific and artistic value.

FLEA CIRCUS

Any old flea will do, but the bigger
the flea, the easier to glue
      it in place or attach a harness.

      Flea foursomes in games of flea whist.
Fleas in dresses and frock coats at a flea ball.
Fleas dressed as Napoleon and the Duke of Wellington.

A single flea pulls an ivory coach
      a flea driver glued to the seat.
A single flea to pull the brass cannon.

Silk-fibre harnesses encircle their necks.

Camphor placed on cotton balls are repellent to fleas.
      They kick them away, become jugglers, ball players.

An orchestra of fleas attached by wire
      to a small music box. When the music plays
the fleas gesticulate to the vibration.
        They are glued to their seats.
      They look like they play musical instruments.

      Below the orchestra, several pairs of fleas are fastened
to each other by a little bar. Pointed in opposite
      directions, each try to get away. Their rotary motion
        is a ludicrous waltz.

By way of finale, L. Bertolotto, the P.T. Barnum of his day
      allows the fleas to sup on his arm.

THE LANGUAGE OF BEES

KARL VON FRISCH, 1886–1982

He falls under their spell in the courtyard
of the institute, but the bees first dance for him
      in a Munich garden.

He loves his bees, warms them in his cupped hands
when the cold stiffens their wing muscles.
      Nurtures them, calls them his little comrades.
He thinks of them as his personal friends.

Is it their profound mystery that allows
him to so deftly snip their antennae, slice
      their torsos, glue weights to their thoraxes, shellac
their unblinking eyes, mutilate their senses
        and manipulate their behaviour?

He believes they test him, challenge him to devise more
      experiments, to learn more. They speak to him
        in the language of dance.

As the honeybee waggle dances, other bees crowd close
      follow its movements, learn where to find
        the nectar and pollen.
He too follows the directions from the hive.

The bees have language, but they never speak.
      He listens. He understands.

VON FRISCH'S *TEN LITTLE HOUSEMATES*

The housefly he calls a trim little creature. A man
would have to leap from the Westminster Bridge

to the top of Big Ben to compete with the flea.
All living creatures are equal in the great law

of life, he writes. Even bedbugs. Lice can carry
two thousand times their body weight with their forefeet.

Cockroaches are a community that has come down
in the world. Silverfish, entirely harmless sugar guests.

The spider's actions differ in detail according to the weaver's
character. In gnats, the organs of flight have reached a high

level of perfection. We cannot blame the tick for her bloodthirstiness.
Anyone who has to hatch a few thousand eggs deserves a good meal.

Moths are useful scavengers. What else would happen
to all the decaying hair and feathers that disintegrate so slowly?

Von Frisch's little housemates are extraordinary, in their own way
exceptional. At the end of each affectionate chapter

he recommends in equally good-natured tone and detail
how each could best be exterminated.

THE PLUME TRADE

During two walks along the streets of Manhattan in 1886, the American Museum of Natural History's ornithologist, Frank Chapman, spotted 40 native species of birds...not flitting through the trees...plucked, disassembled, or stuffed, and painstakingly positioned on...women's hats.
PAUL R. EHRLICH, DAVID S. DOBKIN AND DARRYL WHEYE,
"The Plume Trade"

No unprotected wild species can long escape the hounds of Commerce.
W.T. HORNADAY, 1854-1937

The first time I did it, I was a few miles north of Waldo.
I shot the birds. Pulled out their feathers and ran.
Left the chicks screaming and the adults raw and bleeding
        festering in the blazing sun.

It made me sick. It did. But I got used to it.
The milliners paid me. Feathers worth twice
        their weight in gold.

That French queen, Marie Antoinette
started it, wearing a headdress with feather plumes.
But I've seen whole songbirds stuffed and pinned
        to women's hats.

They told the public that the feathers were shed plumes.
You know, feathers we found scattered on the ground.
        But it wasn't true.

Herons and snowy egrets were the favourites.
I got the best price for feathers from birds
        in the breeding season.

I felt bad at first, leaving the chicks to die.
Killing all the egrets. They say we almost killed off
        all the whooping cranes

but dealers paid well for whole wings of white birds.
Four herons for each ounce of plume. Six egrets
        for the same ounce.

The best was that trip to Laysan Island.
Hundreds of thousands of albatross. Hired twenty-three
        Japanese to kill those nesting birds.

I watched the harvest. They wouldn't leave
their nests. We got six hundred thousand wings that trip.
Just cut them off the living birds and left them to bleed.

I hunted feathers around the world, but it was all over
by the war. Women cut their hair in that new bob style.
Looked like men. They didn't want those big hats anymore.
        Damn shame if you ask me.

TORISHIMA
Bird Island

We watch a film about a volcano, where
        massive flocks of albatross once gathered
            like alabaster lava encrusting
                the slopes of Torishima.

The skies teemed with them
        a constant snowstorm round the island
            a living white pillar that rose from the sea.

They're called gooney birds, you say, because
        of their awkward tumble when they land.
            Because those who came to hunt them
in the millions with baseball bats to make pen quills,
        aigrettes and mattress stuffing, thought the birds
                fools when they didn't flee.

Only small colonies left, you tell me, sparse
        feathery patches sprinkled across
           volcanic rock.

One can almost count the birds. Each descended
        from the handful of albatross at sea
           those years their brethren
                were bludgeoned to death.

Our hands touch in the dark. Your love
for these birds is something silent
        and silver between us.

How white they are against the grey. Black-edged wings.
        Their yellow-stained crowns.
             Their creamy coral bills
                tipped in blue.

SILKWORM

i.   Xi Ling Ji drinks tea

beneath a mulberry tree. A white cocoon drops
     into her steaming cup, its shiny fibre
unwinds, long lustrous filaments
       she wraps around her finger.

Goddess of silk, she weaves the cloth of kings.

ii.   The Chinese guard the secret of silk

for thousands of years. To reveal the secret
     meant death. A princess hides silkworm eggs,
       seeds of the mulberry in her headdress.

Two Byzantine monks return to the west, eggs and seeds
     hidden in the hollow
       of their bamboo walking sticks.

The secret spreads though Europe.

iii.   Once, Chinese women were devoted

to feeding and tending them, to the unravelling,
     the spinning and weaving. An honour
       to raise the silk.

We breed the moths blind and wingless now.
     They are no longer able to live in the wild.

To harvest silk, we boil the worm in its own cocoon.

iv.   In the rooms where they are raised

the sound of silkworms is the sound of rain
     on a bamboo roof.

35

NIGHT MIGRATION

One tragic night more than fourteen hundred lost their lives.
WILLIAM BEEBE, 1877–1962

i.
He knows the night sky, replete with birds.
      Dusk to dawn, they hurry
through the dark. Thrush, warbler,
         vireo. Easier after sundown
      for the woodcock on short rounded wings
         to escape the hawk.

ii.
He wants to count the night birds. Catches the last ferry
      to the Statue of Liberty, watches it carry
the last sightseer back to the city, before he makes
         two trips with blanket, lantern,
food and binoculars up the three hundred and fifty-four steps
      spiralling inside the statue's body, into the crown.
         Climbs the narrow ladder
through her up-stretched arm and emerges
      onto the open-air balcony
         that circles the torch.

iii.
Three hundred feet below, the wakes
      that eddy from tugs and steamers
      in the New York harbour
         look like intersecting strands
         of giant cobwebs.

When night falls, the torch is lit, and the city
      recedes, suspending him in mid-air,
         no contact with sea or land.

The torch sways through a two-foot arc, as if the Lady
will hurl it to the ground. Her hollow body reverberates
with echo like distant thunder.

iv.
Torchlight bells over the harbour.
He can hear more than he can see.

Every few seconds a new chorus of bird calls.
The quok of the black-crowned night heron,
deep gravel of the egret, twitter

of the sandpiper, thin notes of the warbler
and the woodcock's whistle.

A magnolia warbler hurtles past his head, strikes
the torch and falls to his feet.
Through the periphery of light

the birds fly at him in waves, bright
and shiny, like a swarm of golden bees.
They strike the railings and the glass.

He crouches to avoid the collision. In the morning
he will count two hundred and seventy-one
dead birds.

Some cling to him unharmed, wings spread,
heads back, panting.

v.
In the first light of dawn, a herring gull shrieks
toward him from the sea,
swerves sharply,
flies up the river.

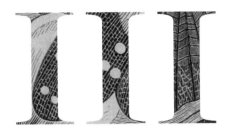

SO FULL
OF GHOSTS

ASCENT

i.
I knew when I saw it rise, a cloud wrapped in silk,
        saw it sail six thousand feet
                in the air, knew

when I saw it descend, skim across open fields chased
        by farmworkers like children
chasing a butterfly, I knew
                I would rise with it, knew
                I would be among the first men
                        to leave the earth and fly.

ii.
When de Rozier convinced the king he was to be
        the first man to go up in an untethered balloon
                I used my wealth
to be the one picked to counterbalance him
        in the circular gallery
                slung below the open neck
                        of the balloon.

iii.
Just above the river Seine at Pessy, across
        from the Champs de Mars, it stood
seventy feet high, a glorious blue
        stitched with golden mythological figures,
                zodiac signs and suns.

The neck of the balloon and an open brazier
        of burning straw so large between us
                I could barely see
                        de Rozier.

iv.

Three thousand feet up
    fluctuating with the wind
        drifting
            across the Seine

swooping the rooftops of Saint-Germain
    we dodged the towers
        of Saint-Sulpice
            rising again

over the woods at Luxembourg
    only to plunge towards the Buttes aux Cailles
        skirting two windmills.

v.

When the wind shook us, I screamed at de Rozier
    to stop
        dancing.

I shouted at him to land the thing
    but he implored me
        to calm myself, enjoy
           the view.

vi.

On land at last, I vaulted from the gallery, sure
    the balloon would collapse and burst
        into flames, but de Rozier

    waited for the golden blue dome to settle
        back on earth, said we'd had enough fuel
           to fly for another hour.

vii.

So many flights after ours. Only ten days later
      the first ascent in a hydrogen balloon.

viii.

We dreamed the wings of Saturn, the eagle of Jupiter,
      the doves of Venus, the peacocks of Juno,
even the winged horses of the sun. We did not want
         to imagine Icarus.

SHOW ME GOD, HIDDEN IN THE STARS
WILLIAM HERSCHEL, 1738–1822

It's Advent, the rising of the quarter moon
when he dares to invade the heavens,
        looks through the eyepiece and falls
in love with a pearl white world, its oceans
        of ancient lava, deep craters and basins.

He is of the moon, the sun high in the lunar sky,
the gibbous moon, where boundary is only light
        and long dark shadow, streamers
flowing river-like, across the crust,
        seas of tranquility, serenity, fertility.

Herschel sees stars as globes rolling through the void
        and he is one of them now
living in that void, imagining this is his world
                his unbound space
        the stars in flux.

Until he pulls away from the telescope, remembers
        he lives on Earth, rooted here by gravity,
                colour and breathing.

FALLING STARS

CAROLINE HERSCHEL, 1750–1848

Every night up on the flat roof
     over the hayloft

the great man's sister
     with her telescope, hunting
       for wanderers
messengers that enter the solar system.

Every night up on the flat roof
     over the hayloft
       in thrall to the polished lens
sweeping the sky for comets.

The great man's sister
     minded the heavens.

No longer such a lonely thing
     to open one's eyes.
Every impulse of light exploding.

Only thirty "hairy stars" ever recorded
     and she, the Lady's Comet Hunter

alone and free up on the flat roof
     over the hayloft
found eight in a dozen years.

She knew those distant stars ceased to exist
     millions of years ago.
Her starry night, her stellar landscape
     not really there at all.

Light travels long
     after the heavenly body is gone.

Her sky, so full of ghosts.

DESCENT

OTIS BARTON, 1899–1992

Our barge slowly rolling high overhead in the blazing sunlight...the long cobweb of cable leading down through the spectrum to our lonely sphere, where, sealed tight, two conscious human beings sat and peered into the abysmal darkness as we dangled...isolated as a lost planet in outermost space.
WILLIAM BEEBE, 1877–1962

i.
As a young boy Barton cuts a length of garden hose,
              weighs himself down with bags of BB shot
and while his brother holds one end of the hose, walks
              down a sloping beach
                        onto the bottom of the sea.

Later he buys a small brass pump, attaches it
              to a plain wooden box inserted with a glass pane,
pulls it over his head. Once again, his brother holds
              pump and hose and once again he makes his descent
                        into the ocean.

ii.
William Beebe, Barton's childhood hero. Acclaimed
              naturalist whose life's work took a sharp turn in 1925
when he donned a copper diving helmet and stepped
down a ladder into the waters of the Galapagos, into a passion
              for the ocean, to know how deep the sea,
              how the ocean floor rose and fell, the nature
                        of life in that total darkness.

iii.
Barton and Beebe on Nonsuch Island, Bermuda.
   The sea, calm. Swells undulate.
     Salt and seaweed mingle with the scent
of begonia. Ancient Bermuda cedars, yellow sedge and golden
   trumpet vines, oleander and hibiscus. The ocean
      stretches as far as the eye can see.

Barton calls his design an inflated
   slightly cockeyed bullfrog.
He and Beebe have to contort their bodies
   to squeeze through the small hatch
     headfirst.

Shoulder to shoulder, two men,
   two oxygen tanks and a palm-leaf fan
to circulate the air. The first human beings
   to descend into the abyss.

iv.
Inside the four-and-a-half-foot bathysphere, out in the open
   Atlantic, Barton sits with his knees drawn
     Beebe back on his heels.
A winch lowers the four-hundred-pound circular door
   into place. Barton's nerves on edge at the hammering
of ten large bolts to shut them in, as if they are secured inside
   a church bell. The turning of the massive wing bolt
     to seal the vessel. Then silence.

Tethered from a mother ship at the surface
   of the ocean by a thin cable
     Barton and Beebe are hoisted up
from the pier, dangled in mid-air. The horizon, the sea
   and the crew below revolve slowly. The sphere
     is lowered into the sea
      until the Atlantic swallows them.

v.
Sixty feet is the depth of the deepest
        helmet dive. Three hundred and six feet,
the deepest dive in a regulation suit. Three hundred
        and eighty-three feet the deepest
submarine. Only dead men have ever reached
        six hundred feet.

Beebe and Barton are lowered over two thousand
        six hundred feet below the surface
of the ocean. The pressure on their three-inch
        window, over six million pounds.
Any molecule of water that enters the sphere would fly
        through their bodies like a high-pressure
                rifle bullet.

vi.
Sunlight shimmers in long rays past their small
        window, and they descend
                through an unearthly cathedral.
The deeper they go, colours disappear until
        even the blues are too faint for naming.

Gaping jaws and needle teeth flash
        through the beam of their searchlight.
Squid and shrimp, pulsating chains of jellyfish.
        Hatchet fish like living light bulbs.
Greys bleach to white until all they see
        are ghost fish.

In the dark, they float on a galaxy
        of bioluminescent sparks.

HALF MILE DOWN

from the journals of William Beebe

No one has ever gone
    so deep, been where light can not
        go. Above us, sponges, shells

and seagrass stick to the bottom
    of the ship that lowers us. The puckered
        surface of the ocean disappears
            as we submerge.

Five hundred feet down, squid
    are silvery brown, fish, blue
        and everything lined with white light.

At eleven hundred feet, dark bodies
    flash by our tiny window. Siphonophores
        strung together like a feather boa

are spun glass in the aquamarine glow.
    A necklace of silvery light. Further down,
        angelfish. Pale lemon tentacles

rise from their heads. An eel like a transparent
    willow leaf. A golden-tailed sea dragon,
        cheeks a bright light.

How red is the first to disappear
    as we descend out of sunlight.
    Then yellow dissolves to green

and how quickly green shifts to blue.
    How the colours vanish
    one by one.

THE GLANVILLE FRITILLARY

ELEANOR GLANVILLE, 1654–1709

Did she think herself mad for her obsession
    with the tumbling motion of
kaleidoscope flight? For wanting to collect butterflies?
    She didn't believe they were the souls of the dead.

Women accused of an unhealthy relationship
    with the natural world still burned at the stake
        as witches. A brave woman then, described
by neighbours as beating the hedges for *a parcel of wormes.*

When she left her husband, he set her children
    against her by claiming she was mad. Surely
for a woman to forsake domesticity for a life of science
    was a sign of insanity.

Her Glanville fritillary spends most of its life
    as a black spiny caterpillar. One of Britain's rarest
butterflies, it lives only a few weeks.
    Orange/brown latticed wings beat rapidly
        before it glides.

THE CARPENTER'S DAUGHTER

The world has used me so unkindly.
Mary Anning, 1799–1847, "The greatest fossilist the world ever knew"

I may have started out lucky, just over a year old
Elizabeth holding me in her arms when the lightning struck
killing her and two other women standing under the elm

but it wasn't lucky to be poor, having to live so close to the sea.
Storms swept the cliffs along the English Channel, flooded our home.
We had to escape out the second-floor window so we wouldn't drown.

The first fossil I found was a pretty ammonite,
a snake stone, and when a tourist paid half a crown
for it, I knew what I had to do.

I didn't understand the fuss at first, just learned
how to find those fossils from my poor da.
I was only eleven when he died.

And dangerous work it was. Crawling under crumbling
cliffs at low tide to find specimens loosened
from the rocks. Best to look for new fossils in winter

when the landslides came, collect them quickly
before they were lost to the sea. I was almost killed once
when a landslide crushed my beloved dog Tray.

But those geologists used me. It was a man's world.
Only twelve when I found the first ichthyosaurus
and later I discovered the first plesiosaur,

vertebrate of marine reptiles, complete skeletons
that made those great men ask themselves –
how could the earth be only a few thousand years old?

I could read and write. I hand copied scientific papers
and studied them. I could identify any bone. Those
professors came to me for help.

I knew more about fossils than anyone. But it was
those fancy gentlemen got all the praise, sucked
my brain and never mentioned me once.

THEY NEVER ASKED ANY QUESTIONS

Annie Montague Alexander, 1867–1950

I'm not after the recognition.
I just want to play a part in solving
the great problems of evolution.
That's the only goal, is it not, of scientific work?

I'm a woman after all, can't vote, supposed to
stay home and look after things.
I have the money to go to those lectures
on paleontology at Berkeley, and I'm thirsty to learn.

It's my money that funds the museum
on campus and my money that pays for the research
the careers of these famous men. My money
funds the field trips and expeditions so I can take part in them.

I work hard on the field trips. Sit in the dust
and sun marking and wrapping bones.
I've contributed thousands
of specimens to the university's collection.

But night after night it's me who stands
before a hot fire, stirs the corn, rice, beans or soup.

I wonder sometimes, if the men think
the firewood drops out of the sky
or whether a fairy godmother brings it.
They never ask any questions.

SILENCE

We who have brought into being a fateful and destructive power.
Rachel Carson, 1907–1964

i.
A winding root-tangled path leads from her cottage
                to tide pools at the shore
clusters of soft coral and fat little sea cucumbers
under layers of mussels and Irish moss.

On summer days she collects periwinkles, anemone, sponges
            barnacles and seaweed, observes the ocean
                current, the loneliness of the North Atlantic.

In the evenings she visits Dorothy, walks the road
            through the fog-shrouded nights.

ii.
How can a woman have such an intelligent
understanding of the physical environment, they ask.

She signs her scientific articles with her initials
so her readers will assume she is a man.

iii.
Three bestselling biographies of the sea
            and *then a rain of death upon the surface of the earth*
                and the sudden silence of birds.

iv.
She warns the world about pesticide threat.

Subversive, antibusiness, pacifist, communist, hysterical –
                                                        a spinster.

We can live without birds and animals, someone wrote,
            but we cannot live without business.

v.
She dies soon after publishing *Silent Spring*.
            She is not yet fifty-seven.
She doesn't live to see the ban on DDT,
            doesn't live long enough to accept
the Presidential Medal of Freedom.

vi.
At the edge of the sea, Dorothy releases
            her ashes to the swell of the waves
watches the birds fly over the blue ocean
                        until the tide turns again.

A CRACK IN THE WORLD

Deep sea soundings...were as a ribbon of light where all was darkness on either side.
Marie Tharp, 1920–2006

Same old story. Women not allowed.
So it was Bruce who boarded the ships, collected
sounding data, and I drew the maps
      the topography of the ocean floor.

The bottom of the sea, a jigsaw puzzle I fit together
latitude by longitude, the ocean no longer
      a flat blue on the map of the world.

I plotted, drew, checked, rechecked
      and I discovered a rift valley along the floor
           of the Atlantic, a forty-thousand-mile
ridge that extended through all the oceans on earth.

Continental drift.
      A crack in the world.

Scientific heresy, Bruce said, girl talk,
      though I knew the rift was real, formed
from where new material pushed up from deep
          inside the earth, split the ridges
      in two, pushed the sides apart.

No one believed in continental drift.
      Pen, ink, rulers. I kept drawing maps
to show them a picture of the rift valley.
      I let them argue

till Cousteau crossed the Atlantic in the *Calypso*
      towing a movie camera on a sled
      along the ocean floor.

Then the boys finally let me onto the boat.

I was the one who found that rift valley.
You could only do that once. You couldn't find
anything bigger than that.

Not on this planet.

SAVING THE WHOOPING CRANE
George Archibald, 1946–

She pined for him
    the dark-haired ornithologist.
When he walked by her pen
    she'd holler and grind.

Tex, one of the last whooping cranes
    and George, the man she fell for

moved in together. He placed his cot
    in her enclosure, wooed her, talked
        to her, foraged

for corncobs and hay with her
    to make their nest.
        And for five springs, they danced.

She'd only dance with him.
    No one else, not even
        her own mate.

Tex, bright red crown, strutted in high step,
    leaped and flapped, stomped her feet,
        tossed her head, trumpeted
            her invitation. And George

in duet beside her, pirouetted
    and bowed, deep knee bends,
        jumping up and down,
            arms spread like wings.

OLD WOMEN IN THE SEA

Off the island of Jeju, where the Yellow Sea meets
     the East China Sea, they say you can hear
          our breathy shrieks and whistles
            before you see us.

In our seventies now, we've been diving
               for more than fifty years.

Sea women, we farm the oceans for abalone, sea urchins,
     octopi, seaweed, shellfish.
            Our men farm the land.

We followed our mothers into the sea. We dove one day
     at a time, and then the days turned to months
          and when we looked up
           we were *haenyo*.

We dive up to eighty times a day,
             even in winter, even if it snows.

We hold our breath for two minutes, dive as deep
     as fifteen metres. If we try to hold our breath
          on land, we cannot. But when we are down
            in the ocean, it just happens.

We are old women, but we are built like the sea. Once
     every girl in every seaside village was *haenyo*,
          every daughter was a diver.

Nothing grows in the ocean anymore. Without shellfish,
          there will be no *haenyo*. No sound of *sumbisori*
     like the cries of dolphins, echoing
             off the seaside cliffs.

MARIA SIBYLLA MERIAN BRINGS
A BRANDIED CROCODILE TO TEA

Maria Sibylla Merian, 1647–1717

i.
a crocodile no bigger than a large insect. Snakes, iguanas
and geckos. Creatures floating in jars of brandy
      to sell as curiosities in the salons
of the rich. She travels alone under the protection
of the captain. The sailors think it bad luck
      to look at her, though they drink her brandy –
            toss her specimens into the sea.

ii.
It begins with silkworms. By thirteen she's etched fifty
      copperplates of caterpillars. No European has yet
          to document their metamorphosis.

The Church preaches all life begins with Creation,
      and scholars believe insects come from
          the spontaneous generation

of rotting mud. Science is a man's game. What woman
      is interested in bugs? Insects are the beasts of the devil
          and witch fever just ended in Germany.

      Painting and drawing not taught to girls either.

iii.
Dead butterflies pinned and preserved
        grow dusty in collectors' wooden
     drawers and cabinets.

What plants had they fed on? Which caterpillars turned
     into glossy moths?

How to interpret an insect that trades
     its home on the earth for one in the air?

She gathers caterpillars from her own garden
       and public parks, studies the life cycles
of the daytime butterflies and the nighttime
     moths, draws the details of their chrysalises
       and the plants they feed on.

          How to understand
the flapping wings, the trajectory of their lives,
     the flight of her own thoughts?

iv.

Thirteen years after Galileo's trial. Before Darwin.
Before Audubon. Before the word *entomology*. Shakespeare
      dead just thirty years. She's fifty-two when she leaves
her husband in Germany to sail to the New World
          on a voyage of science.

V.

Surinam, on the edge
of the rainforest. Everything is strange here. The smell
of boiling cane juice, swamp mud, guava.
Biting ants. The air thick with mosquitoes. The flick
of a black tail in the jungle. Flaming coral adders slip
through the bush at her feet. Her skirts stick to roots,
her hair snags on branches.
The trees shoot skyward,
blue and yellow macaws like bits of sunlight struggling
through the thick dangling vines.

Heat pounds. There is fever and disease and sometimes
she is frightened to breathe.

vi.

She collects every day. Inspects the underside
      of leaves, peers down the long throats of strange white flowers,
searching for caterpillars. Moths with the wingspan
         of a small bird, bright blue lizards,
            pearly iridescent eggs.

vii.

And she paints. Plants and caterpillars once centred
and balanced in watercolours on vellum
spill out the sides of a rough canvas. Her reds from seeds
she soaks in seawater, her blacks from a fruit she presses
then dries in the sun. The pale wood-coloured chrysalis, the butterfly
of polished silver, the morpho with wings like peacock feathers resting
on the roseate flower of a bursting pomegranate.

In the grip of yellow fever, she almost pays with her life.
Her financial future depends on silk cocoons
and dead geckos.

viii.
                              Mid-winter in Amsterdam.
Caterpillars are bound in their cocoons waiting
              for the thaw. To live as an adult, a whole

new body is needed. Inside the squirming larva,
              a precise origami of folding and creasing,
                    a hormonal rising and falling

until it stills like death, an immobile puppet awaiting
              animation. Cells divide, cells die. The pupa
                    will crack, break open. An entire body

will appear where once there was none. Butterfly,
              psyche, breath, soul. Under the snow
                    turtles and frogs are buried

in mud, larvae overwinter under leaves and
              dragonflies sleep under winter ice.

ix.
Something inside her breaks,
        gives in. She closes her eyes. A new birth,
            a hatching, a freeing of breath.

IV

HOW MORTAL
THEY WERE

ENVOY

after Jane Hirshfield

One day in the winter yard, a brown rat
      eating seeds the birds had scattered
            beneath the feeder.

A few days later, a falcon flew off in a huff
      of wing, leaving behind a small pile
            of entrails and tufts of fur.

I don't know if the falcon ate the rat.
      There was no sign of a tail.

All week I watch from the window, on guard
      against possible rat invasion.
            I hold my life on pause

in those moments when I have to look, to see
      if the rat is still there, scuttling
            back and forth between the cedars.

RED

It's a totem, he said. The pileated woodpecker, the sharp clutch
of red on a winter white birch we'd seen at the lake. He saw another flash
of red head in the woods on the drive home.

Back in the city he wrote, it's a bumper crop. His mother saw one
in Ottawa and there was a photo of one on the front page
of the newspaper. He saw one hammer the grey bark
of the mountain ash in his backyard.

My windows are smeared with the ghost smudge
of wings and feathers. Last week a dove broke its neck against
the window and died on the deck. Today a grackle hit so hard
I thought it broke the glass.
I couldn't detect a breath where it huddled on the ground.
Later it was gone.

The raw winter light pushes its way through the cedars, wedges open
what's left of the snow, exposes what's underneath.
Then one weekend, a dozen cardinals
and the next a flock of redwings who shoulder their way
to the bare branches and sing.
One by one, they return to the feeder
only to repeat it all again.

I want to ask him what he meant by a totem. Grackles gather
as the afternoon retreats to twilight, their heads
a glossy purple, their wings aggressive bronze,
iridescent. Their bright golden eyes intent on the cardinals.

I think it's the red
the sudden clarity it brings.

METAMORPHOSIS

A sultry August morning, the sky a wash of amaryllis
        pink and crimson-veined with sunrise. No ripple
            across the surface of the lake.

On the arm of a worn Muskoka chair, I find his hollow
        case and on the path to the lake I find him
chewing his way through the milkweed, his antennae
            like tentacles on the hunt for more food.

The caterpillar undulates, the contractions
        of his four thousand muscles push him towards
his jade chrysalis. I extend my finger and he crawls
           onto the palm of my hand.

I raise him to eye level, watch as he waves his head
        slowly from side to side like a blind man
           tries to sense the distance from palm to leaf.

He will destroy his own body. Only a few cells will remain
        intact inside the pupa, grow into the butterfly
who, one morning, will split his pupal case and eclose.

She plays in fields left unruly, green
   and ripe with weeping willow, buttercup,
milkweed, yarrow and tansy
   before her town sprawls to suburb.
When she holds very still, she can hear
     the plants move.

She catches tadpoles in goldenrod ditches, knows
   the hoverflies and ladybugs, the startle
of long-horned meadow grasshoppers,
     watches them soar, float dreamlike
   when they catapult from her touch
to disappear deep into the tall grass.

She isn't afraid to run her finger over their hard
   shell and sharp wings. She doesn't
recoil from the tickle of their long hind legs
   or the brown juice they spit
     into her hands when she catches them.

She wades through the small riot of yellow rocket
   and wild carrot to coax the grasshoppers
into a jam jar, stuffs too many of them
    into the glass prison

so that they are frantic and angry when she approaches
    the boy who'd looked up her baggy shorts
when she sat on the curb to watch the older kids
    play Skully, that boy
who'd pulled all the buttons off her blouse
    when he grabbed her.

   He is afraid of grasshoppers.

THE KRANSTEIN FOREST

for Edward and Andrea

It was surely one of the last summers
before the wild was tamed
before the weeping willow and maples
in the vacant lots were bulldozed, before
the creeks were bled dry

before the garter snakes left
no trace and the bullfrogs fell
silent, before the monarchs disappeared
though we were reverent with them, never
touched them, fearing to disturb the fine dust
on their wings, believing that would prevent
them from flying.

Our bikes were our horses and every morning
our mothers turned us out the back door
to ride free, and it was the last summer
the three of us, nine or ten years old, rode
further than we had ever ridden before
left the last paved street behind
biked a rough-hewn path we found
for the first time.

It was the last summer
the path we rode opened
onto a wild orchard, masses of pure
white apple blossoms, the scent of heaven.

And it was the last summer
we named our forest, never arguing
about what order to combine our names.
That last summer, it didn't matter
who's name would come first.

FROG

The first time it was a crayfish, bloodless and alien,
beady eyes and antennae like the Martians we watched
on *The Outer Limits*.

We were nervous, yes, but the crayfish was just a thing
to us. It looked like the lobsters we knew
the goyim ate.

But the frog. How we pretended to be more horrified
than we were by what we were asked to do. How
some of us

were probably more repelled than others. One of us
likely rebelled. At least one of us probably puffed up
with false bravado.

And who among us didn't retch at the smell of formaldehyde?
Truth is, more than one of us smoked up before
we entered the lab

toy scientists in our white lab coats, obediently lined up
at our stations, the frogs pinned on their backs, chins in the air,
eyes to the ceiling

creamy lime bellies exposed to our dull blades,
back legs now powerless, front legs upturned
like palms.

There were not enough frogs for the next class to dissect
so we had to sew them back up. I wanted to leave
a message

for the next butcher – penned a tiny note and attached
it like a flag to what I thought was
probably the pancreas.

Ribbit.

MORNING GLORY

We were in high school, so we couldn't
grow weed ourselves and we were always
            on the lookout for some
way to get high. We considered poppies,
but an interest in gardening would have raised
            suspicion and anyway we didn't have
                    the patience.

One of us read about morning glory seeds
and I was chosen to buy several packets
            from Vincelli's Landscape Company
            around the corner.

Vincelli was also our neighbour.
            He lived three doors down, and while
he was used to seeing me walk my dog
                    past his house and past his nursery
he would be surprised to see me come
            inside to buy something.

I was more than a little scared of Vincelli
            whose business spanned the blocks
between the CN tracks and the corner of our street
            leaving an unlit sidewalk
down his long fence, where I would walk
            our dog and where, high up in a tree
                    you could see a moose head
            he'd nailed to the top of the trunk.

So I brought the dog into the store with me
            bought ten packets of seeds. No one
batted an eye. Later, after we'd baked the seeds
                    rolled them and smoked them
and I vomited violently all night
            it was the dog who stayed up with me
watching balefully, waiting for his six a.m. walk.

TERRARIUM

We had the best intentions
        didn't we? We travelled
by city bus over an hour through a bitter
        winter night to get the cage
            for free. Our canary Ché,
        so cheerful and alive until
we left our front door open while we sat
on the porch, saw the neighbour's cat slink
            out, orange feathers in his mouth.

We decided to collect fish. Filled an aquarium
        like an electric dollhouse
a phantasmagoria of life we couldn't
        take our eyes from, until we found
the coral swordfish, curled like a comma
        on the wooden floor.
                  No matter how often
we rescued him, he jumped again.

When we split up, I convinced you
        we made better friends than lovers.
I persuaded you to stay.

We used our empty aquarium and built
        a green ecosystem we knew
nothing about, to make a home for an iguana.
        It took two weeks for the flora
to flourish and two and a half
        for the fauna to die.

GINKGO

There was one in front of the Arts Building
and rumour had it, the oldest tree
in North America, the last one
     and maybe we believed
          it was true. But it wasn't.

It was, as it turns out, a living fossil, a link
to the age of dinosaurs, part of a single species
     with no living relative, unchanged
for over two hundred million years
     but they grow in cities everywhere.
          There was even another one
     on campus, at the Faculty of Law.

It was an exotic tree to us, so different
     from the regal border of elm
edging the road leading up from the Roddick Gates
          to the Arts Building. The leaves
were fan shaped, finely pleated, golden, elegant.
     And the fruit smelled like vomit.

And while the sugar maples took their time
every fall, turning colour, shedding their leaves
     over weeks, the ginkgo held on
to its incandescence, dropping its leaves suddenly
     all at once, in synchronicity.

The only species in the world to lose its leaves all at once.
We never saw it happen, though we took bets on the date.

One day every fall, they were just gone.

TADPOLES

They used to be everywhere
      when I was growing up
in Côte-Saint-Luc, a town not yet a suburb.

Now, like the golden frogs in Panama,
      the Sierras, Costa Rica, Ecuador
all the tadpoles are gone

and so are the wildflower meadows
      and the ditch at the end of my childhood
street we were told not to go near
      the warning only drawing us closer, thrilled
to be shinnying down the steep embankment
      to the meandering stream that trickled there.

I caught tadpoles in that creek
      tried hard to grow them into frogs
in a metal pail in my garage.

I was in thrall to the story
      that Egyptians believed frogs
came from the coupling of land and water
      when the Nile flooded every year.

They never survived
      their tadpole state
and every day I discovered another death
      by the smell in the garage.

Gone the baritone call of the bullfrog
      the small wetland outside my door.

MUSCA DOMESTICA

I kill them. Arms outstretched I carry
the dead on plastic fly-swatter gurneys, dump them
                    outside the back door.

My father made a sport of it, stalking
            them from behind, scooping them
up in his hand. Flies, quick and alert
            to our every move, he caught
in his palm, one at a time.

He told us that if a pair began to breed
            in April and all their progeny lived,
by August they'd carpet the earth, stacked
                    forty-seven feet deep.

    I liked to observe them when I was a kid,
chin on folded hands. I didn't know I was watching
            them excrete and vomit on the food
                    we left uncovered. I didn't know
they thrive where we thrive, survive where we fail,
            didn't know about disease, about the future
                    and what it could bring.

SWEET

Our house in the suburbs
        had a backyard, a front yard –
land – land that was his. My father, a son
        of Russian immigrants, poor all their lives
was the first in his family to own property.

No one would mistake his house
          for anyone else's. He painted
      the foundation a light blue. He laid the stones
of his front walk on a curve, not a straight path like
          the other houses, stained them coral pink.

He wanted to plant. For the generations before him
        sweetness came only from the flesh of fruit.

Cherry and plum trees flourished near the corner
          of the porch, raspberry canes smothered
      the east wall of the house in cloying abundance
but his pride was the apple tree that thrived
         in the centre of the backyard.

Five types of apples grew on that tree. He pruned it,
       fertilized it. Baskets and baskets of apples
         we didn't know
            what to do with.

WHITEFISH

I don't think I understand the poetry
in Gerald Stern's fourteenth collection
      but all that talk about kasha and varnishkas
drives me into the kitchen to consider
what he wrote about Ezra Pound
           while I search for something Jewish
to eat, and all I can find is a jar of gefilte fish
left over from Passover, which makes me think instead
      about whitefish, smoked, and my father
who, on those Sunday mornings in Montreal
         when he was in a good mood
      would drive to our local deli to buy the fish.
And how, for our breakfast, he would painstakingly
        remove every tiny bone.

TULIPS

i.

They say that during the Ottoman Empire, the Turkish sultan
      had a passion for tulips.

For weeks each spring, he filled his imperial gardens
      with hundreds of thousands of tulips.

Tulips with petals that opened too widely, he had
      hand-stitched shut with fine thread.

Between the flowers in the earth, thousands more
      were placed beside them in exquisite cut glass.

Beside every tulip, long slender tapers were set
      into the ground and lit.

Hundreds of giant tortoises, candles on the shells
      of their backs, lumbered through the gardens.

Songbirds held forth from gilded cages. Mirrors placed
      around the gardens enhanced the display.

Once a night a cannon sounded, the doors to his harem opened
      and his mistresses stepped out, led by eunuchs bearing torches.

The extravagance of the sultan's tulip festival is said
      to have been the downfall of his rule.

ii.
My father pursued a variegated tulip. Not the deep red or dark
        purple of the parrot tulip, not the delicate fringed

edges of the pink fancy frill. No, he had an obsession
        for a tulip striped red and yellow

colours that made me ill to look at, reminded me
        of eggs and ketchup.

In spite of their colour, his tulips were cool and aloof
        where they lined up like soldiers in his front garden.

Every year he pursued that variegated tulip. Every year
        they were less and less hardy.

He didn't know that the vigour of a variety fades with time.
        He didn't know how mortal they were.

MAYFLY

for R

Once, though I'd just been given
        six months to live, you told me
I couldn't die because you weren't done
            with me yet.

We were sitting side by side on my back steps
        under the wisteria, the spring not quite given
over to summer, my garden an ethereal wash of mauve

            and though I may not remember much
of what people have said to me over the years,
        I remember that.

But it was you, in the end, who was alive
        for what seems to me now like mere days.

      You always wanted to be
ephemeral, your long narrow body to be filled
        with air, never having to have to eat or drink.

When I heard you were dying, I imagined you
        fallen to the water's surface, paralyzed,
            open-winged.

I wanted to believe you found freedom from suffering.
      I wanted to believe you floated on the wind,
           that final dissolution,
               into clear light.

ACKNOWLEDGEMENTS

Thanks to the journals where several of these poems first appeared, sometimes in an earlier form: *The Fiddlehead, Grain, Prairie Fire, Event, CV2, The Antigonish Review, The Dalhousie Review* and *Queen's Quarterly.*

The poem "Maria Sibylla Merian Brings a Brandied Crocodile to Tea," which first appeared in *Grain*, was a finalist for a National Magazine Award in 2014.

The poem "Darwin's Orchid" was a finalist for the *Malahat Review*'s Open Season Award in 2015.

Thanks to the Banff Centre for Literary Arts for the time I was able to spend there in a self-directed residency.

Thanks again to my writing group – Marilyn Gear Pilling, Dick Capling and Ross Belot – for our weekly go at these poems.

Thanks to Robert Hilles for the edit.

And as always, thanks to Ken for his love and unwavering support.

"Nabokov's Blues"

While Vladimir Nabokov is best known for his fiction and criticism, he was equally distinguished as an entomologist. His interest in the field was inspired by the books of Maria Sibylla Merian. During the 1940s, as a research fellow in zoology, he was responsible for organizing the butterfly collection of the Museum of Comparative Zoology at Harvard University. The genus *Nabokovia* was named after him in honour of this work, as were a number of butterfly and moth species. Though his work was not taken seriously by professional lepidopterists during his life, new genetic research supports Nabokov's hypothesis that a group of butterfly species called the *Polyommatus* blues came to the New World over the Bering Strait in five waves.

"Darwin's Orchid"

The hawk moth, discovered in 1882, twenty years after Darwin's death, is so rare, feeding only at night, that it was not witnessed feeding on the Madagascar orchid until 2011, when it was caught on film with infrared light.

"Cage"

Ota Benga (1883–1916) was a Congolese man, an Mbuti pygmy known for being placed in the controversial human zoo exhibit at the Bronx Zoo in 1906. He committed suicide in 1916 at the age of thirty-two.

Sarah Baartman (1789–1815) was one of at least two Khoikhoi women who, due to their large buttocks, were exhibited as freak show attractions in nineteenth-century Europe under the name Hottentot Venus. *Hottentot* is now considered an offensive term.

"The Language of Bees"

Karl von Frisch (1886–1982) shared the Nobel Prize in 1973 for finding that bees communicate the distance and direction of a food supply to other members of the colony by two types of rhythmic movement, or dance.

"Ascent"

On November 21, 1783, Pilâtre de Rozier and the Marquis d'Arlandes were the first human passengers in a free-flight Montgolfier balloon. Ironically, the first human passenger was also the first victim of balloon travel. Pilâtre de Rozier was killed on June 15, 1785, when his balloon, filled with a combination of hydrogen and hot air, crashed during an attempt to fly across the English Channel.

"Show Me God, Hidden in the Stars"

Sir Frederick William Herschel (1738–1822) was a German-born British astronomer, composer and brother of Caroline Herschel. He discovered the planet Uranus in 1781, and as a result of this discovery, George III appointed him Court Astronomer.

During his career, he constructed more than four hundred telescopes. The largest and most famous of these was a reflecting telescope that has come to be called the Herschelian telescope. In 1789, he discovered two new moons of Saturn.

"Falling Stars"

The line "every impulse of light exploding" belongs to Adrienne Rich from her poem "Planetarium."

The line "no longer such a lonely thing to open one's eyes" also belongs to Adrienne Rich from her essay "When We Dead Awaken: Writing as Re-Vision" from the book *On Lies, Secrets, and Silence.*

Caroline Herschel (1750–1848) never married, but served as her brother William Herschel's assistant until his death. She was the first woman to discover a comet, ultimately finding eight. She also discovered several deep-sky objects and was the first woman to be given a paid scientific position and to receive an honorary membership into the Royal Astronomical Society.

"Descent"
William Beebe (1877–1962) was best known as an American
naturalist and ornithologist. His interest in marine biology
led to his 1930s dives in the Bathysphere with its inventor,
Otis Barton. These dives set several records for the deepest
dive ever performed by a human, the deepest of which stood
until it was broken by Barton fifteen years later.

"The Glanville Fritillary"
Eleanor Glanville (1654–1709) remains one of only two people
to have a native British butterfly named after them. Her family
attempted to contest her will by Acts of Lunacy because
"none but those who were deprived of their Senses, would
go in Pursuit of Butterflies."

"The Carpenter's Daughter"
Mary Anning (1799–1847) was a British fossil collector and
paleontologist whose finds along the English Channel at Lyme
Regis in the county of Dorset in southwest England contributed
to major changes in scientific thinking about prehistoric life.

"They Never Asked Any Questions"
Annie Montague Alexander (1867–1950) was an American
philanthropist and paleontologist who established the University
of California Museum of Paleontology (UCMP) and the Museum
of Vertebrate Zoology (MVZ), and financed their collections, as
well as a series of paleontological expeditions. She took part
in many of these expeditions, gathering a significant collection
of fossils. Some of her words in this poem were taken from her
letters found on the UCMP and MVZ websites.

"Silence"
Best known now for her book *Silent Spring* (1962), Rachel Carson (1907–1964) was also the bestselling author of several other books about the sea – *Under the Sea Wind* (1941), *The Sea Around Us* (1951) and *The Edge of the Sea* (1955).

"A Crack in the World"
Marie Tharp (1920–2006) was an American geologist, oceanographer and cartographer, who, with Bruce Heezen, was the first to scientifically map the entire ocean floor. Tharp's work revealed the presence of the Mid-Atlantic Ridge, causing a paradigm shift in earth science that led to the acceptance of the theories of plate tectonics and continental drift.

"Saving the Whooping Crane"
George Archibald (1946–) was born in New Glasgow, Nova Scotia, and is the co-founder of the International Crane Foundation. He spent three years acting as a male crane with an endangered whooping crane named Tex to encourage her to reproduce and eventually Tex did succeed in laying a fertile egg.

"Old Women in the Sea"
The word *haenyo* means sea women. Haenyo are female divers in the Korean province of Jeju.

"Maria Sibylla Merian Brings a Brandied Crocodile to Tea"
Maria Sibylla Merian (1647–1717) was a German-born naturalist and scientific illustrator. Her observations and documentation of the metamorphosis of the butterfly is considered one of the most significant contributions to the field of entomology.

Linda Frank was born in Montreal and now lives in Hamilton, Ontario. She has written three books of poetry: *Cobalt Moon Embrace, Insomnie Blues* and *Kahlo: The World Split Open*, which was shortlisted for the Pat Lowther Award. She is a past winner of the Banff Centre's Bliss Carmen Poetry Award and has been shortlisted for the National Magazine Awards.